I have enjoyed being a close personal friend of Robert Scrivner for more than twenty years and for a goodly number of those years had the privilege of being his pastor. Early in our friendship I recognized that besides being able to write in meter and verse, Bob has a very profound understanding of New Testament theology.

I feel others will be very pleased with Robert's *Good News Poetry*. I wish him very good success in relating his understanding of scripture while staying true to his love for rhyming metered verse. Perhaps others, by Bob's success, may be inspired to pursue the pleasure of poetic endeavors.

—Reverend Sherwood Vegsund

GOOD NEWS TRILOGY

The Gift
Gospel Poems
In Faith and Victory

Robert Scrivner

LUCIDBOOKS

THE GIFT

Contents

The Gift

Justification / vindication!
Christ Jesus spanned the rift;
And Luther nailed it to the door,
That heaven is God's gift.

Love thesis from the heart of God—
God's liberation plan.
Our Lord alone has paid the price,
To ransom captive man.

We thank you, Martin Luther,
For God's great grace explained;
The law and prophets showed us sin . . .
And Christ for us was slain.

The wage of sin is total death,
That lasts for e'er and e'er;
But ours THE GIFT . . . eternal life,
By simple sinner's prayer.

A Poetic Meditation of Romans 5:15–17; 2 Corinthians 9:15 (AMPC)

But God's free gift is not at all to be compared to the trespass [His grace is out of all proportion to the fall of man]. For if many died through one man's falling away (his lapse, his offense), much more profusely did God's grace and the free gift [that comes] through the undeserved favor of the one Man Jesus Christ abound *and* overflow to *and* for [the benefit of] many.

Nor is the free gift at all to be compared to the effect of that one [man's] sin. For the sentence [following the trespass] of one [man] brought condemnation, whereas the free gift [following] many transgressions brings justification (an act of righteousness).

For if because of one man's trespass (lapse, offense) death reigned through that one, much more surely will those who receive [God's] overflowing grace (unmerited favor) and the free gift of righteousness [putting them into right standing with Himself] reign as kings in life through the one Man Jesus Christ (the Messiah, the Anointed One).

Now thanks be to God for His Gift, [precious] beyond telling [His indescribable, inexpressible, free Gift]!

By Jesus's Blood Applied

I am a son of God,
By Jesus's blood applied;
For when He rose to heaven,
God hailed the Crucified:

"Welcome home, My Faithful,
Your blood has cleansed their sin;
Your sacrifice the total price,
To make them whole again."
If you would be God's son,
Don't thrust His gift away . . .
Your Father pleads from heaven,
"Receive My love today!"

A son of love by blood,
For all eternity—
God's gift to all who kneeling call,
"Put Jesus's blood on me!"

A Poetic Meditation of Hebrews 9:12 (AMPC)

He went once for all into the [Holy of] Holies [of heaven], not by virtue of the blood of goats and calves [by which to make reconciliation between God and man], but His own blood, having found *and* secured a complete redemption (an everlasting release for us).

Each Child He Counts So Dear

God's grace is truth that we must share;
He wants His world to hear.
For He loves us as His own,
Each child He counts so dear . . .

That He would send His own to die
For a thankless, sin-filled race.
To those He loved, He sent His Son.
They spit in Jesus's face.

They plucked His beard and harshly placed
Fierce thorns to pierce His brow;
While Father wept, "Of righteous sons,
I'll have a billion now.

"Washed fully clean in crimson stream,
That flows from Savior's side;
All who come I'll count as Mine—
Not one will be denied.

"If they who've sinned and jeered,
To mock My Son to shame,
Will humbly bow, I'll hear them now,
And save in Jesus's name."

A Poetic Meditation of Mark 15:17, 19 (AMPC)

And they dressed Him in [a] purple [robe], and, weaving together a crown of thorns, they placed it on Him. And they struck His head with a staff made of a [bamboo-like] reed and spat on Him and kept bowing their knees in homage to Him.

Eternal Grace

I'm going home to reign with Christ,
For I've received eternal life.
Reborn to serve my Sovereign Lord,
Eternity is my reward.

The blood of Jesus ransomed me,
And by this gift I'll ever be
Fully free from sin's domain,
And of the found of Calvary's slain.

No merit but Christ's blood alone . . .
By grace I'll kneel at heaven's throne;
Through tears of joy to view His face,
The Lamb of God—eternal grace.

A Poetic Meditation of Ephesians 2:8, John 3:16 (AMPC)

For it is by free grace (God's unmerited favor) that you are saved (delivered from judgment *and* made partakers of Christ's salvation) through [your] faith. And this [salvation] is not of yourselves [of your own doing, it came not through your own striving], but it is the gift of God.

For God so greatly loved *and* dearly prized the world that He [even] gave up His only begotten (unique) Son, so that whoever believes in (trusts in, clings to, relies on) Him shall not perish (come to destruction, be lost) but have eternal (everlasting) life.

Eternal Life

Eternal life is mine today,
And when I die, so then;
For Jesus Christ, the Lord of life,
Has given life to men.

Once bound by sin—assailed by death—
I had no life in me;
But Christ, the ever-living God,
Arose my life to be.

Now, I've the life of heaven,
Beginning on this earth;
For Jesus Christ—eternal life—
Is mine at second birth.

A Poetic Meditation of Ephesians 2:8 (AMPC)

For it is by free grace (God's unmerited favor) that you are saved (delivered from judgment *and* made partakers of Christ's salvation) through [your] faith. And this [salvation] is not of yourselves [of your own doing, it came not through your own striving], but it is the gift of God.

God's Grace

God's grace this day is pleading,
"Your heart now give to Me.
I bore your sin to give you life,
With love eternally."

Two thieves on crosses, made their choice—
You, too, must do the same.
Hell's death reject God's grace elect!
Choose life in Jesus's name!

"Today with Me in paradise!"
The promise . . . one believed;
And without sin he entered in,
For grace his prayer received.

A Poetic Meditation of Romans 6:14, Luke 23:43 (AMPC)

For sin shall not [any longer] exert dominion over you, since now you are not under Law [as slaves], but under grace [as subjects of God's favor and mercy].

And He answered him, Truly I tell you, today you shall be with Me in Paradise.

The Gospel

The gospel means glad tidings,
To men of every race:
"God loved enough to bear your sins—
Christ Jesus took your place!"

Though wrath of God toward sin meant death,
Your penalty Christ bore;
That God might count you without sin—
Redeemed forevermore.

To good news kneel . . . submitting,
To God who gave you breath . . .
Then rise to reign forever free,
With Him who canceled death.

A Poetic Meditation of Romans 1:16 (AMPC)

For I am not ashamed of the Gospel (good news) *of Christ*, for it is God's power working unto salvation for deliverance from eternal death] to everyone who believes *with* a personal trust *and* a confident surrender *and* firm reliance, to the Jew first and also to the Greek.

In God's Eternal Grace

Four billion hands . . . two billion hearts,
Before the throne of God;
Love anthems raise to Christ who paid
Their ransom by His blood!

Once captive held by Satan's lies,
The truth has made them free.
Now without sin, because of Him,
They sing eternally:

"We thank You, spotless Lamb of God,
For leaving heaven's throne,
To shed Your precious holy blood,
To make us Father's own.

"For by no works of righteousness,
Have we attained this place;
But time now past, we stand at last,
In God's eternal grace!"

A Poetic Meditation of 2 Corinthians 8:9 (AMPC)

For you are becoming progressively acquainted with *and* recognizing more strongly *and* clearly the grace of our Lord Jesus Christ (His kindness, His gracious generosity, His undeserved favor and spiritual blessing), [in] that though He was [so very] rich, yet for your sakes He became [so very] poor, in order that by His poverty you might become enriched (abundantly supplied).

Jesus! Blessed Jesus!

I hear His praise in a baby's cry;
I view His love in a mother's eyes;
I know His might in the lightning skies;
The lilies lift His glory high!
He is Jesus! Blessed Jesus!

Our Lord of love—the God of peace—
Grants mercies new at day's release;
And golden grains resound increase,
In sustenance that shall not cease . . .
From Jesus! Blessed Jesus!

He's source of light and life for all,
The helping One who lifts our fall
And salves heart tears, great and small;
He's Sovereign Lord on whom we call . . .
Christ Jesus! Blessed Jesus!

He's Lamb of God, our King who came,
To grant new life and grace to claim.
Let all the earth extol His fame!
The Creator God—as Savior—came.
He is Jesus! Blessed Jesus!

A Poetic Meditation of John 1:4 (AMPC)

In him was Life, and the Life was the Light of men.

Jesus Is the Savior

Take courage—kneel to Jesus Christ—
    He will your prayer receive,
      For Jesus is the Savior,
    To hearts that will believe.

He rescues from deception,
    Makes spirit eyes to wake;
    And gives the Holy Spirit,
    To guide each step you take.

Receive God's love in Jesus,
    Don't wait a moment more;
    Let heaven's Son of mercy,
    True peace and love restore.

A Poetic Meditation of 1 Timothy 4:1 (AMPC)

But the [Holy] Spirit distinctly *and* expressly declares that in latter times some will turn away from the faith, giving attention to deluding *and* seducing spirits and doctrines that demons teach.

KING

We see Him bow . . . a battered King . . .
Mocked with thieves—cast out.
(And men of "learning"— yet, as then,
Today hurl spears of doubt).

This King of kings is humble.
All might of power is His;
Yet beneath the sign, by men maligned,
His life for theirs He gives.

King of the Jews and Son of God,
(Two crimes; one sign; no sin);
To prove the sign to death resigns—
A ransomed realm to win.

Jesus of Nazareth—King of the Jews—
As King shall rule the earth;
But until then, He pleads with men:
"Receive My gift—new birth.

"Plucked out of hell's dark kingdom,
Accept your special place,
As son and heir to blessing,
In the kingdom of God's grace."

A Poetic Meditation of John 19:19, 21 (AMPC)

And Pilate also wrote a title (an inscription on a placard) and put it on the cross. And the writing was: Jesus the Nazarene, the King of the Jews. Then the chief priests of the Jews said to Pilate, Do not write, The King of the Jews, but, He said, I am King of the Jews.

Kingship

No greater power on earth there is,
Than glorious truth that Jesus lives.
No other King to set us free,
But Jesus Christ of Calvary.

This King was born to die despised,
Then rise the King for e'er.
And we may crown Him as our own,
In humbled-sinner's prayer.

He heeds each plea of bended knee—
Bowed hearts He makes anew.
He is the King for every heart,
That counts His kingship true.

A Poetic Meditation of Romans 10:9 (AMPC)

Because if you acknowledge *and* confess with your lips that Jesus is Lord and in your heart believe (adhere to, trust in, and rely on the truth) that God raised Him from the dead, you will be saved.

Life Crown

It's not by blood of bulls and goats
That I've received life's crown;
But by the blood of Christ the Lamb,
From heaven's throne come down.

For though the judge of man God came
To bear my debt for sin;
And when I bowed His grace to claim,
My heart was born again.

Life's crown received from heaven's King,
Love's rapture floods my soul;
And my heart glad cannot be stilled,
But Jesus's worth extol.

A Poetic Meditation of Hebrews 9:14 (AMPC)

How much more surely shall the blood of Christ, Who by virtue of [His] eternal Spirit [His own preexistent divine personality] has offered Himself as an unblemished sacrifice to God, purify our consciences from dead works *and* lifeless observances to serve the [ever] living God?

Love Divine

Such glorious—wondrous—love divine,
That we should be His own.
God's gift of grace, our confidence,
And access to His throne.

For by His blood He made us sons,
And placed His life within.
That we as His ambassadors,
Might shine His love to men.

A Poetic Meditation of 2 Corinthians 5:20 (AMPC)

So we are Christ's ambassadors, God making His appeal as it were through us. We [as Christ's personal representatives] beg you for His sake to lay hold of the divine favor [now offered you] *and* be reconciled to God.

Majestic Beauty

I am an heir to heaven bound,
  For God has promised me,
By the blood of His dear Son,
  His glorious face to see.

Bright gems of earth, that glimmer rare,
  Are pale in heaven's light;
And glow of fame and wealth shall fade,
  To ashes at the sight . . .

Of God Almighty on His throne,
  Before His ransomed throng,
Attired in glistening robes and crowns,
  To sing their Savior's song.

No diamond in the universe
  Has beauty like our Lord—
JESUS CHRIST, the flawless Lamb,
  By His redeemed adored.

A Poetic Meditation of Revelation 4:2–3 (AMPC)

At once I came under the [Holy] Spirit's power, and behold, a throne stood in heaven, with One seated on the throne! And He Who sat there appeared like [the crystalline brightness of] jasper and [the fiery] sardius, and encircling the throne there was a halo that looked like [a rainbow of] emerald.

New Creation One

Three days beneath the earth . . .
Then with a mighty stroke,
Father brought Him forth in might . . .
As the gates of hell Christ broke.

Shackled by the chains of sin?
Your bonds He'll break away,
As you kneel your heart,
And call His name today.

If this day you call to God,
He will not turn aside.
Jesus's blood removes all sin,
To make you clean inside.

Twice born you'll stand again,
God's new creation one—
Not patched nor renovated,
But *new* in Christ the Son!

A Poetic Meditation of 2 Corinthians 5:17 (AMPC)

Therefore if any person is [ingrafted] in Christ (the Messiah) he is a new creation (a new creature altogether); the old [previous moral and spiritual condition] has passed away. Behold, the fresh *and* new has come!

New Kings

New Israel means new kings with God,
For sovereign blood brought birth;
And we shall reign with Jacob's slain,
In victory's glorious mirth.

The day of Christ's appearing roars
Above the clamored throng;
And we shall raise on earth His praise,
One thousand years of song.

Sing praises to earth's sovereign Lord—
By heaven's crown we're saved;
And never shall our sins be named,
For Father's love forgave.

Once bowed beneath our guilt of sin,
We knelt to choose God's cure;
And sins removed, stand reconciled
Since Jesus's blood washed pure.

A Poetic Meditation of 1 John 1:7 (AMPC)

But if we [really] are living *and* walking in the Light, as He [Himself] is in the Light, we have [true, unbroken] fellowship with one another, and the blood of Jesus *Christ* His Son cleanses (removes) us from all sin *and* guilt [keeps us cleansed from sin in all its forms and manifestations].

No Sin Separating

Jesus preached the good news—
God's kingdom come to men—
Forgiven and restored,
As if we'd never sinned.

No sin separating,
From Father's loving care;
With God made one again,
By contrite-sinner's prayer:

"Father God, I'm sorry for
The wretched things I've done.
Cleanse my soul and make me whole,
By blood of Christ, Your Son."

A Poetic Meditation of Romans 10:9 (AMPC)

Because if you acknowledge *and* confess with your lips that Jesus is Lord and in your heart believe (adhere to, trust in, and rely on the truth) that God raised Him from the dead, you will be saved.

Nothing Less . . . Nor More

Without the cross it is a cult—
No matter what they preach.
Man's "righteous" deeds, **unrighteous** deemed,
Shall never heaven reach.

Your best can't purchase heaven!
It's just Christ's blood, you see,
That cancels sin to let you in,
To reign with majesty.

When your last journey you begin,
Your destination is set,
And every act except the cross,
The Father must reject.

So put your trust in Jesus Christ,
To gain you heaven's shore.
It is your repentance and His blood—
Nothing less . . .nor more.

A Poetic Meditation of Luke 24:47 (AMPC)

And that repentance [with a view to and as the condition of] forgiveness of sins should be preached in His name to all nations, beginning from Jerusalem.

On This Road to Glory

I've found God's way to heaven—
I've heaven in my soul—
And on this road to glory,
The waves of glory roll.

Come! Join me on this journey;
Make Jesus Christ *your* King.
Then let's together gather,
That other souls might sing . . .

The joy of God's redemption—
The peace our Lord imparts—
And love's overflowing fountain,
When Jesus rules the heart!

A Poetic Meditation of Matthew 9:37–38 (AMPC)

Then He said to His disciples, The harvest is indeed plentiful, but the laborers are few. So pray to the Lord of the harvest to force out *and* thrust laborers into His harvest.

The Only Light

Jesus left the throne room,
Where Father's love shines bright.
He freed me from hell's bondage,
And made my darkness light.

No longer in dark night I dwell
(from heaven's light denied).
For Jesus Christ illumes my soul,
And by His Spirit guides.

Come bow with me before God's throne;
Make Jesus Christ your Lord.
Deceiver's deathful lies reject.
Choose freedom in God's Word.

Repent—now turn your back on sin—
And daily walk God's way.
For Jesus is the *only* light,
That shines to heaven's day!

A Poetic Meditation of Acts 13:47, Romans 10:9 (AMPC)

For so the Lord has charged us, saying, I have set you to be a light for the Gentiles (the heathen), that you may bring [eternal] salvation to the uttermost parts of the earth.

Because if you acknowledge *and* confess with your lips that Jesus is Lord and in your heart believe (adhere to, trust in, and rely on the truth) that God raised Him from the dead, you will be saved.

Redemption

How can I ere convey to you,
Redemption as it is?
My spirit once by sin made dead,
Reborn by blood now lives!

My Jesus went to the marketplace,
Where sin slaves were chained.
He purchased me with His own blood.
Once lost . . . I've been reclaimed!

Now I'm bound to Savior's heart,
By crimson cords of care.
Now I approach the throne of God
And find my Father there.

A Poetic Meditation of Ephesians 1:7 (AMPC)

In Him we have redemption (deliverance and salvation) through His blood, the remission (forgiveness) of our offenses (shortcomings and trespasses), in accordance with the riches *and* the generosity of His gracious favor.

Redemption's Song

I long to sing **Redemption**—
Our Savior's special song.
That one that we'll be singing,
The endless ages long.

It is a regal anthem,
To heaven's majesty,
Our Savior's song of triumph—
Salvation victory!

We shall sing before the angels,
Redemption's joyous verse.
Our song of adoration,
To Him who bore sin's curse:

"No other One is worthy,
But Lamb on David's throne!
Christ Jesus is **Redemption**,
And by His blood we're home!"

A Poetic Meditation of Luke 1:32, Hebrews 9:12 (AMPC)

He will be great (eminent) and will be called the Son of the Most High; and the Lord God will give to Him the throne of His forefather David.

. . . not by virtue of the blood of goats and calves [by which to make reconciliation between God and man], but His own blood, having found *and* secured a complete redemption (an everlasting release for us).

Righteous

If you built a Babel tower,
Of the good works you have done,
You'd be a billion miles beneath,
The holy of God's Son.

If you sacrificed your lifeblood,
To attempt to salve your sin,
You in self-righteous rags would be,
Unclothed . . . ***un*born again**.

So God's holy Son descended,
From His throne room to the earth,
To live a sinless life and die,
To buy for *you* **new birth**.

God's gift of grace . . . ***His*** righteousness;
At Calvary's cross lay claim,
To the righteous work of Jesus,
And receive His robe and name.

A Poetic Meditation of Romans 6:13 (AMPC)

Do not continue offering or yielding your bodily members [and faculties] to sin as instruments (tools) of wickedness. But offer *and* yield yourselves to God as though you have been raised from the dead to [perpetual] life, and your bodily members [and faculties] to God, presenting them as implements of righteousness.

Saint John 3 Meditation

You are a triune being—
Spirit, body, and soul.
God's perfect plan since time began,
That you in Him be whole.

For born of flesh is flesh alone,
But of Spirit . . . life divine;
And born again means death-doomed men
Can live as God designed.

As Moses placed the serpent high,
God likewise His Son raised;
That those He loved—with sins removed—
Might reign His triune race.

With Nicodemus know the truth,
That truth one night expressed.
By blood of Christ—God sacrificed—
Eternal life possess.

A Poetic Meditation of John 3:14–16 (AMPC)

And just as Moses lifted up the serpent in the desert [on a pole], so must [so it is necessary that] the Son of Man be lifted up [on the cross],

In order that everyone who believes in Him [who cleaves to Him, trusts Him, and relies on Him] may *not perish*, *but* have eternal life *and* [actually] live forever!

For God so greatly loved *and* dearly prized the world that He [even] gave up His only begotten (unique) Son, so that whoever believes in (trusts in, clings to, relies on) Him shall not perish (come to destruction, be lost) but have eternal (everlasting) life.

Song of Salvation

Dear Savior, You promised,
As You walked this earth,
To take to Your home,
Each child of new birth.

The streets of that city of love,
Will be bright,
With Your glory, our God,
For You are the light.

Life river will sparkle,
Through life's healing trees:
No death, sorrow, crying,
Nor pain—only peace.

Our great loving Father
All tears will erase,
And ever we will praise Him,
Who died in our place.

Crucified, risen,
And reigning above;
The King of all ages,
Redeemer through love!
Our song of salvation,
All heaven will flood:
**"Hallelujah, forever . . .
BOUGHT BACK BY HIS BLOOD!"**

A Poetic Meditation of Revelation 22:1–2 (AMPC)

Then he showed me the river whose waters give life, sparkling like crystal, flowing out from the throne of God and of the Lamb Through the middle of the broadway of the city; also, on either side of the river was the tree of life with its twelve varieties of fruit, yielding each month its fresh crop; and the leaves of the tree were for the healing *and* the restoration of the nations.

Today . . . Be Born Again

Bow at the feet of Jesus Christ;
God's love your heart will fill.
Christ's blood—life-giving fountain—
Is flowing to you still.

Let love fountain your heart cleanse;
Christ's blood takes sin away.
Forgiveness is forever yours,
If only "Yes!" you say.

Be reconciled to Father,
With home on heaven's shore.
Know total restoration,
By Jesus's blood outpoured.

Forgiveness sent from heaven,
Is flowing for all men.
Receive redemption mercy—
Today . . . be born again!

A Poetic Meditation of Acts 20:28 (AMPC)

Take care *and* be on guard for yourselves and the whole flock over which the Holy Spirit has appointed you bishops and guardians, to shepherd (tend and feed and guide) the church of the Lord *or of God* which He obtained for Himself [buying it and saving it for Himself] with His own blood.

To Heal Man's Fall

To Moriah's mount, the Prince now comes,
To make of men, God's righteous sons.
To ransom men, and sins atone,
The press of wine, He treads alone.

He's Son of God, and Son of Man;
He's Christ the Lord, and Christ the Lamb.
He to serve, lays glory down,
To lift men up, to wear His crown.

The peace men seek, Jehovah brings,
In Son of David, the suffering King.
For with His blood, the fallen to claim,
Jehovah God here bears sin's shame.

Jehovah's love, Messiah shows,
That men who bow, might freedom know.
Yahweh the Son—sovereign of all—
New covenant cuts, to heal man's fall.

A Poetic Meditation of Acts 1:6 (AMPC)

So when they were assembled, they asked Him, Lord, is this the time when You will reestablish the kingdom *and* restore it to Israel?

The Worth of Man

He who formed the world in might,
Finds in man His heart's delight.

No other creature on the earth,
Bears God's mark, nor has such worth;
That God would cause His Son to die,
To cleanse the wayward's guilt thereby.

The worth of man . . . God's love revealed,
By act of grace on Calvary's hill.
The blood of God, the price for men,
As heaven's King there bore their sin.

Now all who come to Christ to cleave,
Repentance speak, their sins to leave;
And claiming Jesus as *their* Lord,
By act of grace arise restored.

A Poetic Meditation of Ephesians 2:8 (AMPC)

For it is by free grace (God's unmerited favor) that you are saved (delivered from judgment *and* made partakers of Christ's salvation) through [your] faith. And this [salvation] is not of yourselves [of your own doing, it came not through your own striving], but it is the gift of God.

Yeshua the Lamb

May your name be inscribed in the Book of Life,
Forever by your King.
May you in the blood of Yeshua Lord,
Escape from death's cruel sting.

From the lake of fire may your soul be saved,
By Mashiach's cleansing flood.
From Immanuel's veins your redemption came,
And your only hope . . . His blood.

Yeshua Hamashiach is the sacrifice,
That canceled all your sin.
By His blood to the door of your life applied,
In Lamb's Book of Life be penned.

Yeshua the Lamb—friend of Abraham—
Is the Lord of all mankind.
In that final day when every spirit prays,
Will He in His book *you* find?

A Poetic Meditation of Revelation 20:15 (AMPC)
And if anyone's [name] was not found recorded in the Book of
Life, he was hurled into the lake of fire.

Your Life

Lord, You built Your universe.
You breathed **Your** life in man.
You shared with him Your ownership.
Then gave Your rescue plan.

(When the best of Your creation—
In Your own image formed—
Your paradise by sin had plunged,
To anguish and discord.

You looked into our darkest night,
And saw us groping there;
Then shed in love redeeming blood,
To heal our deep despair.)

Lord Creator, God of grace,
Who chose our death for sin,
Remove sin-debt and by Your breath,
Grant us **Your** life again.

A Poetic Meditation of Genesis 2:7 (AMPC)

Then the Lord God formed man from the dust of the ground and breathed into his nostrils the breath *or* spirit of life, and man became a living being.

GOSPEL POEMS

Contents

Adams

The serpent's lie, God's first man chose—
He disobeyed God's Word—
And righteous garments sin-dissolved,
Gained sin-chains and discord.

O, Adam, how you've fallen low,
Like Lucifer before;
For through your sin you've ushered in,
Hell's torments, lies, and wars.

No daily face to face with God—
Communion is constrained,
And though God gave the promised seed,
We wrestle sin and pain.

First Adam became first child of sin.
The second Adam is Christ;
Now for all men is found in Him,
God's sin-cure sacrifice.

Now Adams new may know God's love,
When they choose grace for sin . . .
And bow before God's cure for sin,
To rise to life in Him.

A Poetic Meditation of Genesis 3:6 (AMPC)

And when the woman saw that the tree was good (suitable, pleasant) for food and that it was delightful to look at, and a tree to be desired in order to make one wise, she took of its fruit and ate; and she gave some also to her husband, and he ate.

Adoration

Beyond earth's temporal wealth,
Or universal fame,
There glows eternal beauty rare—
Christ Jesus is His name.

When Jesus rules the spirit,
Full rapture floods the soul.
Once you've viewed His glorious face,
Earth's diamonds seem dull coal.

There is naught of earth can turn aside,
From heaven's golden strands;
When Jesus Christ, the Lord of lords,
Your ransomed heart commands.

A Poetic Meditation of Luke 2:21 (AMPC)

And at the end of eight days, when [the Baby] was to be circumcised, He was called Jesus, the name given by the angel before He was conceived in the womb.

Aints

Aints are those who do not have,
A future blessed and bright.
They live each day as castaways,
From eternal life in Christ.

Aints are lost! They cannot win—
Though pinnacles they climb.
Each fleeting high, to aint heart cries,
"Where lives true peace of mind?"

Aints ain't saints. They do not choose,
To find life's greatest thrill.
Aints Jesus shun . . . they lonely run . . .
They never live fulfilled.

A Poetic Meditation of Colossians 1:12 (AMPC)

Giving thanks to the Father, Who has qualified *and* made us fit to share the portion which is the inheritance of the saints (God's holy people) in the Light.

Architect Divine

The stars and moon the night illume . . .
The sun brings forth the day.
If the heavens spoke in rhyme,
This to us they'd say:

"Our order is no accident,
What fools some mortals be.
It was no chance cosmic happening,
But plan of Majesty."

Building grand and beautiful,
Bespeaks architectural mind.
Boundless, celestial canopy,
Cries forth . . . Architect divine!

On canvas of silent splendor,
Creator majestic speaks.
As intellect thirsts for wisdom,
Wisdom His most loved seeks.

Wisdom says, "Not nothingness,
On vast cosmos sea;
But created in My image . . .
Sons of Majesty."
Yes! The heavens declare God's glory,
And we shall do the same;
For we are the sons of God,
By might of Jesus's name!

A Poetic Meditation of Psalm 19:1–4 (AMPC)

To the Chief Musician. A Psalm of David.

The heavens declare the glory of God; and the firmament shows *and* proclaims His handiwork.

Day after day pours forth speech, and night after night shows forth knowledge.

There is no speech nor spoken word [from the stars]; their voice is not heard.

Yet their voice [in evidence] goes out through all the earth, their sayings to the end of the world. Of the heavens has God made a tent for the sun.

Armageddon Victor

True Armageddon battle—
When white-robed armies ride—
God's justice meting skirmish,
As Bridegroom leads His bride.

This famed "war of the ages"
Shall hardly be a fight,
For this Victor is the sword of truth,
That severed hell's dark night.

He is King of kings! He is Lord of lords—
Earth's Victor in a day!
By spoken word from His own mouth,
Shall the valley flow a bay.

Fowls swiftly fly to gather flesh,
Of captains great, made small;
As Armageddon Victor speaks,
Millennial peace for all!

A Poetic Meditation of Revelation 19:19 (AMPC)
Then I saw the beast and the rulers *and* leaders of the earth with their troops mustered to go into battle *and* make war against Him Who is mounted on the horse and against His troops.

Asleep 'Til Gehenna Lake

Asleep—not awake—they slumber,
Not knowing where they are.
The streets are full of vision-dull,
Bound, sins-tied, for brim of hell . . . not far!

What warning can these spirit-dead hear?
How can their slumber cease?
How shall the dead-in-spirit awake,
Before they die asleep?

A love tap on the shoulder,
Will not their spirits awake.
"Bridge out ahead!" Who will wake spirit-dead?
We must, to forever-vision shake.

The gospel-gun jab in their rib.
Cock the hammer! Jolt forever awake!
Those dying spirit-dead are eternally dead—
Hades kept 'til Gehenna Lake!

A Poetic Meditation of Romans 13:11 (AMPC)

Besides this you know what [a critical] hour this is, how it is high time now for you to wake up out of your sleep (rouse to reality). For salvation (final deliverance) is nearer to us now than when we first believed (adhered to, trusted in, and relied on Christ, the Messiah).

Because He Asked

He was a five-day Christian,
Who Monday chose God's grace;
And Saturday at four p.m.,
Met Jesus face to face.

Dad found the love God promised,
When he gave Christ control;
And Jesus's blood, because he asked,
Redeemed forever his soul.

A Poetic Meditation of Luke 23:43 (AMPC)

And He answered him, Truly I tell you, today you shall be with Me in Paradise.

Behold the Lamb of God

Jesus is the Lamb of God,
Of whom the Scriptures speak.
Repent, believe, and follow.
He is that One you seek!

He comes forth from the Father,
With healing in His wings.
God's Spirit is upon Him;
Deliverance might He brings.

Holy Spirit descending,
And lighting as a dove;
Father's seal of Sonship rests,
Upon this Prince of love.

See Him on Golgotha's cross,
Redeeming you from sin.
See His paschal blood flow down,
To make you whole again.

A Poetic Meditation of John 1:29 (AMPC)

The next day John saw Jesus coming to him and said, Look! There is the Lamb of God, Who takes away the sin of the world!

Blood Covenant Provisions

Blood covenant provisions, Christ Jesus secured;
Much greater than those, provided in first.
Blood Covenant Lamb—living—is Jesus the Word;
And His seven-place bleeding, dismantled sin's curse.

In the Garden of Eden, dominion was lost;
But Gethsemane garden preceded the cross.
In this garden of prayer, sweat-blood Jesus spilled;
And blood covenant included, the freeing of will.

At the whipping-post cruel, our Savior's back peeled.
And in faith—by these stripes—our diseases were healed.
Then crown of thorns piercing, made Jesus's brow bleed;
Now in faith—by this bleeding—from lack we are freed.

From the pain of hands-nailing—with bleeding—
Christ writhed;
Now our hands in endeavors, gain blessing of Christ.
Blood flowed from His feet, from the spike wedged in;
Now we in faith treading, our inheritance win.

From the spear in His side, flowed water and blood;
And His broken-heart death, each hurting heart floods . . .
With cleansing of memory, and healing through love.

Christ's seventh-place bleeding—harsh bruising for sin—
Was binding iniquities, removing within.
And the temple-veil torn, from the top to the floor,
Means God and His man, are together once more.
Jesus cried from the cross, "It is finished—completed!"
By blood covenant provisions, the devil is defeated.

A Poetic Meditation of Hebrews 8:8 (AMPC)

However, He finds fault with them [showing its inadequacy] when He says, Behold, the days will come, says the Lord, when I will make *and* ratify a new covenant or agreement with the house of Israel and with the house of Judah.

By Blood of Calvary's Lamb

When the sands of time slip final,
Gently through the glass;
When time gives place to "everness"—
It is justice bar at last.

A verdict will be given.
That judgment will be true.
For angels are recording,
If God's book you're subject to.

There, all books will be opened;
All sins shall be revealed.
In that moment of your hearing,
Time shall speak and not conceal.

Only sins by blood forgiven,
Receive no mention there.
All others will be blaring,
"This one prayed no sinner's prayer!"

Will you embrace the Savior now,
That His blood might melt your sin?
In this, God's day of mercy,
In Lamb's Book of Life be penned . . .

"That from sands of ancient desert,
'Neath the cross near Western Wall,
To the judgment seat of heaven,
Messiah's blood might call:

"Count these ransomed, worthy—
They obeyed God's first command—
They searched the Scriptures 'il they found,
And bowed to Calvary's Lamb.

"In My blood upon the doorpost,
Passover they receive;
They looked upon My bleeding brow,
And viewing love, believed . . .

"That I received sin-suffering—
Your salvation plan to make—
That they might make decision,
To reject the devil's lake.

"These chose Your great redemption—
Not hell's writhing with the damned—
And, Father, they are Your children,
By the blood of Calvary's Lamb."

A Poetic Meditation of Revelation 20:12 (AMPC)

I [also] saw the dead, great and small; they stood before the throne, and books were opened. Then another book was opened, which is [the Book] of Life. And the dead were judged (sentenced) by what they had done [their whole way of feeling and acting, their aims and endeavors] in accordance with what was recorded in the books.

By Blood of Christ

Only by the blood of Christ,
Shall any ransomed be;
Only in His crimson washed,
Shall any heaven see.

The Word of God our witness . . .
His testimony sure;
Only by the blood of Christ,
Shall we o'er hell endure.

Though tribulation tumult,
And steeped oppression come;
Much assailed we shall prevail,
By blood of Christ the Son.

A Poetic Meditation of 1 John 1:7 (AMPC)

But if we [really] are living *and* walking in the Light, as He [Himself] is in the Light, we have [true, unbroken] fellowship with one another, and the blood of Jesus *Christ* His Son cleanses (removes) us from all sin *and* guilt [keeps us cleansed from sin in all its forms and manifestations].

By Blood Redeemed

Mounding, bounding, flowing down,
There streams from heart of heaven's Crown,
God's grace unfettered . . . love unbound;
To make of men His holy ground.

For on the brow of Calvary's hill,
Heaven's Crown His lifeblood spilled;
And now His crimson floods the earth,
To cleanse from sin and bring new birth.

Yes! On a cruel cross Jesus our king,
Yielded self . . . new life to bring;
And souls sin-bound by love were spared,
As "Blood redeemed!" God's grace declared.

A Poetic Meditation of John 3:3 (AMPC)

Jesus answered him, I assure you, most solemnly I tell you, that unless a person is born again (anew, from above), he cannot ever see (know, be acquainted with, and experience) the kingdom of God.

By Might of God

By might of God the Spirit,
In blood of Christ we see;
A cleansing, healing fountain flow,
To set the captives free.

By might of God the Spirit,
Vile sickness fetters fall,
When sons of God hear Father's heart,
And in the Spirit call . . .

The blood of Jesus faithful,
The love of God unchanged;
And might of grace-dominion shared,
Still dwelling in the name . . .

Of Him whose death sin curse did break,
Salvation full to bring.
And spirits, minds, and bodies heal . . .
The healer—Christ the King!

A Poetic Meditation of Revelation 1:5 (AMPC)

And from Jesus Christ the faithful *and* trustworthy Witness, the Firstborn of the dead [first to be brought back to life] and the Prince (Ruler) of the kings of the earth. To Him Who ever loves us and has once [for all] loosed *and* freed us from our sins by His own blood.

The Call

Will the city be shaken to the roots . . . to the core?
Yes truly! Yes fully! When saints come to war.

Who will surrender their choice and their plans?
The souls of the city you hold in your hands.

Who will give daily the rest of their lives?
These questions seek answers, your actions provide.

Rise early and seek Me; your decision declare.
The call of My Spirit: "Now seek Me in prayer!"

A Poetic Meditation Proverbs 8:34, Luke 10:2 (AMPC)

Blessed (happy, fortunate, to be envied) is the man who listens
to me,
watching daily at my gates, waiting
at the posts of my doors.

And He said to them, The harvest indeed is abundant [there is
much ripe grain], but the farmhands are few. Pray therefore the
Lord of the harvest to send out laborers into His harvest.

Calling

Generation of fig trees, obey My command.
Bring forth ripe figs a sign to My land.
Announce My arrival; I come as their King.
My praise on your lips, as deliverance you bring.

The first time I came, My compassion was known.
Today just as then, I plead for My own.
I'm calling forth laborers into My field.
It is you I am calling. I want you to yield.

Bow to My Spirit, as His breezes are blowing,
Gently bending the branches where ripe figs are growing.
The gifts of My Spirit flow through you this hour,
Demonstrating My love; showing forth My power.

Abide in Me as My words live in you;
Surrender your will, My will to do.
I am the vine, I nourish My branches;
My limbs I make strong, as My army advances.

The time of the harvest nearly is past.
This harvest today . . . reap as the last.
My coming is quick, then all will be lost.
Enter My harvest fields, whatever the cost.

A Poetic Meditation of Matthew 24:32–33 (AMPC)

From the fig tree learn this lesson: as soon as its young shoots become soft and tender and it puts out its leaves, you know of a surety that summer is near.

So also when you see these signs, all taken together, coming to pass, you may know of a surety that He is near, at the very doors.

Calvary's Fount

Please forgive. I've sinned so much,
And laughed Your Son to shame;
But now I come with contrite heart,
To ask in Jesus's name:

"Take away this guilt that tears,
Within my heart and soul;
Wash me clean in precious blood,
That I might be made whole."

For in blood-fount on Calvary's mount,
The debt for sin was paid—
To bring men out of hell's dark night,
To God's eternal day!

A Poetic Meditation of Romans 6:23 (AMPC)

For the wages which sin pays is death, but the [bountiful] free gift of God is eternal life through (in union with) Jesus Christ our Lord.

Children in This Night

As a mourning in the evening,
God hears their tortured pleas;
As men of sin in vilest whim,
Abuse the flesh of these.

For servants of the darkness prince—
In human flesh arrayed—
The sweet and tender hearts and minds,
Of heaven's loved betray.

That **evil has an origin,**
This sordid sin conveys;
As victims of hell's pervert-prince,
Hell's wickedness display.

O men of love and mercy, rise . . .
The vile of heart remove;
And to the children in this night,
True love of Jesus, prove.

A Poetic Meditation of Matthew 19:14 (AMPC)

But He said, Leave the children alone! Allow the little ones to come to Me, and do not forbid or restrain or hinder them, for of such [as these] is the kingdom of heaven *composed*.

Choose Life

Mighty are God's chosen—man.
Dominion is theirs . . . God-given;
Yet when they live apart from Christ,
In *truth* they are not living.

Only man through reasoning,
Can choose the love of God;
Only man knows hope of heart,
Beneath the chastening rod.

Only man can rise above,
Depression and disease;
Only man can choose to serve,
Earth's Sovereign on their knees.

Mighty men of valor all,
Who choose the life of Christ;
For naught of earth is net enough,
To snare abundant life.

A Poetic Meditation of Deuteronomy 30:19 (AMPC)

I call heaven and earth to witness this day against you that I have set before you life and death, blessing and the curses; therefore choose life, that you and your descendants may live.

Choose Today the Christ

Father issues His *final-laborers* plea:
"Come all who trust My Word.
Believers, in faith go forth to reap!
Harvest 'grain' for Christ your Lord!"

Today, Christ calls out to His own:
"Raise now the dead! Heal now the sick!
Come every man to My *final crop*!
Behold! My coming is quick!

"In My Spirit armor clothed, go forth.
Proclaim My sacrifice.
Call all mankind to know God's love,
As they bow to Me, the Christ.

"Exhort the lost, 'Come all! Be saved!
Avoid earth's darkest night!
Tribulation war is at the door.
Heed LOVE's *last-hour call*!
Choose today the Christ!'"

A Poetic Meditation of Luke 10:2 (AMPC)

And He said to them, The harvest indeed is abundant (there is much ripe grain), but the farmhands are few. Pray therefore the Lord of the harvest to send out laborers into His harvest.

Come to the Altar of Freedom

The Spirit of the Lord is alive in this place.
He is calling you now. His freedom embrace.
Jesus is the Savior. There is no other name.
His salvation is free. His wholeness now claim.

The altar is open. Jesus's blood flows free.
It is time to be free in His full liberty.
The song is residing. The offer is now.
Final minutes tick. Come to Jesus. Here bow.

You have heard the gospel story before,
But still you are alone without Jesus.
There are many in hell today who fell,
Rejecting living blood that frees us.

Come to the altar of freedom from pain.
Rejoice in the Lord. Be free in His name.
Father's offer is fleeting. Do not be lost.
Know Jesus as Savior. Experience Pentecost.

A Poetic Meditation of Galatians 5:1 (AMPC)

In [this] freedom Christ has made us free [and completely liberated us]; stand fast then, and do not be hampered *and* held ensnared *and* submit again to a yoke of slavery [which you have once put off].

Commission

Who will rise to bear My love,
To those not yet My own?
I'm seeking soldiers called by blood,
To draw men to My throne.

Who will kneel to hear My voice,
And rise to heed command,
To spread the good news of My grace,
In each and every land?

Redeemed by blood to sonship,
And kept by grace, now be . . .
Anointed servants Spirit sent,
To draw all men to Me.

A Poetic Meditation of Acts 1:8 (AMPC)

But you shall receive power (ability, efficiency, and might) when the Holy Spirit has come upon you, and you shall be My witnesses . . .

Commissioned Rhyme

He calls them songs of deliverance,
And themes of majesty.
He asks me if I'd like to scribe,
His love poetically.

So pen in hand I write them down—
These gentle words I hear—
That all who choose may know His love,
And bow in reverent fear.

He always speaks of Calvary,
And worth of men He sought;
He tells me too of mansions bright
For those His crimson bought.

"Robert! Robert! write it plain!
Declare this truth for Me,
There is no sin too vile or mean,
Not cleansed at Calvary."

A Poetic Meditation of Ephesians 5:19 (AMPC)
Speak out to one another in psalms and hymns and spiritual songs, offering praise with voices [and instruments] and making melody with all your heart to the Lord.

Commissioned to Obey

Come into My chamber, son.
Sit here by My side.
I love you, son, I love your poems,
My Spirit will provide.

Listen well. Obey Me, please.
Declare the good I say.
You are to Me love poetry,
I am with you all the way!

Bow before My written Word.
In metered rhyme declare,
All My love and majesty,
I am with you everywhere.

Rise and stand for righteousness,
Redemption, love, and grace.
Be My pen to lead all men,
Into My freedom place.

A Poetic Medication of Ephesians 5:19 (AMPC)

Speak out to one another in psalms and hymns and spiritual songs, offering praise with voices [and instruments] and making melody with all your heart to the Lord.

Covenant of the Lamb

By sacrifices Israel gained,
Blood *covering* for their sins;
But in the blood of Christ the Lamb,
Our every guilt is *cleansed*.

When Jesus died on Calvary's cross,
Sin-*covering* covenant ceased;
And now in *cleansing* blood of Christ,
We are from guilt *released*.

No more shall God remember wrongs,
That we were guilty of;
For in God's covenant of the Lamb,
Sin *leaves* in Jesus's blood.

A Poetic Meditation of Acts 3:19 (AMPC)

So repent (change your mind and purpose); turn around *and* return [to God], that your sins may be erased (blotted out, wiped clean), that times of refreshing (of recovering from the effects of heat, of reviving with fresh air) may come from the presence of the Lord.

Crimson-Ransomed Theme

As men and angels waiting kneel,
Before the throne of God,
The angels ask, these home at last,
Of ransom by Christ's blood.

"The mystery, in our God once hid,
Is now our lasting peace;
And in the kingdom of our Lord,
We nevermore shall cease . . .

"To sing of God's eternal love,
His mercy and His might,
Which brought us out of dark domain,
To never-fading light.

"We celebrate together here,
The victory of our King;
And journeys done exalt the Son,
In crimson-ransomed theme:

'Worthy is the Lamb to know,
Our everlasting love—
To be adored by men restored,
By His redeeming blood!'"

A Poetic Meditation Psalm 8:4–6 (AMPC)

What is man that You are mindful of him, and the son of (earth-born) man that You care for him?

Yet You have made him but a little lower than God [or heavenly beings], and You have crowned him with glory and honor.

You made him to have dominion over the works of Your hands; You have put all things under his feet.

Crown Christ Lord

Bow to Jesus! Crown Christ Lord!
Alive in Him, lift up your sword.
Let His words of liberty

In your mouth bring victory.
In His light arise to be,
A faithful son of Majesty.
Forever freed—salvation living—
All laud, all praise, to Jesus giving!

A Poetic Meditation of Psalm 91:16 (AMPC)

With long life will I satisfy him
and show him My salvation.

Don't Be a Faith-fake

Don't be a faith-fake—silence-fooled—
Moved from faith to mental assenting.
Voice-stilled by fear, faith wilts and dies.
Standing mute, is to Satan's thefts consenting.

The two great sides of faith include
Being *fully persuaded* and *speaking*.
Telling God's truth while twisting your boot,
O'er the center of Satan's thieving.

Dominion-ones wear God's armor well,
Love's sword from their spirit wielding.
To *spoken,* mature, full-grown faith,
Christ-defeated demons still are yielding.

Since YHWH rent earth-temple veil,
His freedom-shofar *sound*.
Releases sin-captives to freedom this hour.
Slay mental assent. Resurrect your faith.
Faith *strongly speaks* Christ's defeat of hell—
Declaring to all Love's power!

A Poetic Meditation of Mark 11:23 (AMPC)

Truly I tell you, whoever says to this mountain, Be lifted up and thrown into the sea! and does not doubt at all in his heart but believes that what he says will take place, it will be done for him.

Easter Jubilation

Jesus's tomb is empty! It's bare!
Rabboni Yeshua is gone.
As Jesus told us, His Father
Excitedly welcomed Him home.

On the third day, He has risen,
Just as our Savior had spoken.
King of the Jews, He is alive!
Hades defeated . . . Satan's might broken!

Resurrection morning victory!
Great celebration—glad joy!
Sin-slaves no longer, all sickness behind.
Liberated tongues, great rejoicing, employ.

Since exaltation of Jesus to heaven,
Tremendous freedom now abounds.
Globe-circling song of redemption rehearse.
Let Easter jubilation worldwide resound.

A Poetic Meditation of Luke 24:7 (AMPC)

That the Son of Man must be given over into the hands of sinful men (men whose way or nature is to act in opposition to God) and be crucified and on the third day rise [from death].

Easter Morning Jesus

On Easter morning, Jesus the Christ
Came forth in splendored radiant might,
Though we'd no chance to honor Him dead.
His rising grandeur our praise did ignite.
We had come early before the dawn.
We sought the place where He was laid.
We would have honored with fragrant spice.
At His tomb we would have highest regard conveyed.
There at His grave we would have knelt.
There we'd have exalted His name rightly.
Then through the garden He came . . .
Jehovah the Son.
There Jesus was forever our spirits delighting.

Highest honored from Calvary
Jesus sweetly came.
Hades behind Him, He would to heaven soar.
As Messiah I AM, God's sacrificed Lamb,
This Easter morn, Jesus we highly adored.

We worshiped Jesus,
His resurrection might we acknowledge.
We gave highest honor to God's risen Lamb.
As He asked we touched Him not.
For He would ascend to His Father our Lord Jehovah I AM.

Easter morning praises we will lift
To our ascended Savior, Yeshua, Lord supreme.
We will give eternal worship to God's holy Son.
For by His blood we are forever redeemed!

A Poetic Meditation of Luke 24:1 (AMPC)
But on the first day of the week, at early dawn, [the women] went
to the tomb, taking the spices which they had made ready.

Easter Triumph

Easter means that God above,
Held nothing back in proving love.
For when at first His man rebeled,
God's love for sons determined hell,
Would be repaid for anguish caused,
When His own Son would mount the cross,
To bear the sins of all mankind,
By bruise of back and blood divine.

Easter is God's triumph hour,
When Christ arose the greater power.
For hell rejoiced at Friday's plight,
But greatly quaked at Easter's sight;
As myriad sons like Abraham,
In one great host with Christ the Lamb,
Ascended free of "planned abyss,"
When Spirit crushed hell's haughty hiss.

Easter means the victory is won,
And skirmish wins rest with God's sons.
For gates of hell on Easter swang,
Open wide at voice that rang:
"Arise, My Son! Arise, great Child!
Your blood so pure has reconciled,
Every son of faith that dies,
Trusting in Your sacrifice."

A Poetic Meditation of Revelation 1:18 (AMPC)

And the Ever-living One [I am living in the eternity of the eternities], I died, but see, I am alive forevermore; and I possess the keys of death and Hades (the realm of the dead).

Echoes from the Ark

While Noah stood upon the deck,
To make God's plea each night,
The crowds laughed loudly,
"Where's this rain of horror that's our plight?"

And still today "great men of thought,"
Loudly jest with scorn:
"There is no God, nor fire of hell;
No Gabriel, and no horn!"

Though echoes from the ark resound,
From pulpits in the land,
These men of "higher learning" scoff,
The wrath of God at hand.

Yet wailings of the drowning throng,
Once taunting Noah's plea,
Constrain again . . . LOVE's plea to lift,
"Flee to the ship of heaven's Majesty!"

A Poetic Meditation on John 3:5 (AMPC)

Jesus answered, I assure you, most solemnly I tell you, unless a man is born of water and [even] the Spirit, he cannot [ever] enter the kingdom of God.

IN FAITH
AND VICTORY

Contents

Faith and Victory

We walk in faith and victory,
In Jesus Christ our Lord.
His might confirms what we affirm,
As written in His Word.

We pray and say what Father says . . .
God's written will we heed.
As we believe we have received,
Our Father meets our need.

We are the ones who overcome . . .
God's Word our victory plan.
By blood of Christ—love sacrificed—
We pray, we speak, we stand.

A Poetic Meditation of 1 John 5:4 (AMPC)

For whatever is born of God is victorious over the world; and this is the victory that conquers the world, even our faith.

Anointing

Anointing is God's might transferred—
The power to do God's will—
And as we love as Jesus loved,
Anointing flows to heal.

Commissioned by the Nazarene,
The truth of God we share;
And as we speak as Jesus spoke,
Anointing . . . love declares.

Compassion with anointing joins,
To heaven's throne of grace;
And as we preach God's written will,
Confirming signs take place.

A Poetic Meditation of 1 John 2:27 (AMPC)

But as for you, the anointing (the sacred appointment, the unc-
tion) which you received from Him abides [permanently] in you;
[so] then you have no need that anyone should instruct you. But
just as His anointing teaches you concerning everything and is
true and is no falsehood, so you must abide in (live in, never depart
from) Him [being rooted in Him, knit to Him], just as [His anoint-
ing] has taught you [to do].

Assurance

Trust in Me with all your heart.
Believe My Word is true.
For I have given promise,
And surely I shall do!

Each jot and every tittle,
Of My Word won't pass away.
I'm Jesus Christ, your Lord of love,
And I uphold this day.

I'm of My church . . . commander!
I'm captain of angel hosts!
My might, My own, now dwells in you,
By the precious Holy Ghost.

Seek first our Father's kingdom;
Be faithful to My task.
I know your every need,
Before you think to ask.

You are My greatest pleasure,
For My kingdom dwells in you.
Keep in your heart My promise;
I'm Amen . . . Faithful . . . True!

A Poetic Meditation of Revelation 3:14 (AMPC)

And to the angel (messenger) of the assembly (church) in Laodicea write: These are the words of the Amen, the trusty *and* faithful and true Witness, the Origin *and* Beginning *and* Author of God's creation.

Awake! Arise!

The time is short, to midnight creeping;
Shake yourself—arise from sleeping.
Awake! Arise! Most faithful one,
There's kingdom work that must be done.

A few more days of healing power,
Then comes for earth her darkest hour.
Soon comes the night of Jacob's trouble;
Quickly now, the cadence double.

My mighty name knows no defeat;
My marching host does not retreat.
Cry the cry within the street,
"Awake! Arise! Your King to meet!"

A Poetic Meditation of 1 Thessalonians 5:6 (AMPC)

Accordingly then, let us not sleep, as the rest do, but let us keep wide awake (alert, watchful, cautious, and on our guard) and let us be sober (calm, collected, and circumspect).

Believe

Abba Father looks from heaven,
His love on you to shine.
Be brave, be strong, be vigilant;
It is His will divine.

You are His new creation,
A love-adopted son.
He wants you strong to conquer;
You need not ever run.

Believe that God still listens;
Believe that He still acts.
Don't let doubters change your mind;
Just trust God's simple facts.

This God who never changes,
Is living strong in you.
You are His new creation;
Believe His Word is true.

A Poetic Meditation of Luke 8:50 (AMPC)

But Jesus, on hearing this, answered him, Do not be seized with alarm *or* struck with fear; simply believe [in Me as able to do this], and she shall be made well.

By Faith I See

Satan laughs and circumstance,
Joins him in his game.
Yet they can't steal the joy I know,
Through faith in Jesus's name.

I prayed, believing I received,
That which I desired;
And time nor hell can ever quench,
The hope God's Word inspires.

I know by faith that I shall see,
Deliverance in my Lord;
For earth and heaven are sustained,
By God's eternal Word.

A Poetic Meditation of Mark 11:24 (AMPC)

For this reason I am telling you, whatever you ask for in prayer, believe (trust and be confident) that it is granted to you, and you will [get it].

Caleb Faith

Young Caleb went out walking,
To see what he could see;
And with the eye of faith,
He saw the victory.

Faith viewed his Canaan home,
With vineyards growing there;
Then braced his heart with courage,
Dispelling doubt's despair.

Ten voiced their opposition strong,
In blaring doubt-report;
Yet, "In God's might made able!"
Was this mountain man's retort.

Though majority opinion,
Filled fainting hearts with fear;
"Young" Caleb saw those giants felled,
For forty faith-filled years.

Jehovah's strength is conquest might—
Strong faith viewed vineyards gains—
For fervent tread of faithful soles,
Sees every giant slain.

A Poetic Meditation of Numbers 14:6–8 (AMPC)

And Joshua son of Nun and Caleb son of Jephunneh, who were among the scouts who had searched the land, rent their clothes,

And they said to all the company of Israelites, The land through which we passed as scouts is an exceedingly good land.

If the Lord delights in us, then He will bring us into this land and give it to us, a land flowing with milk and honey.

Child Faith

The faith of a child is simple.
What Father says is true.
If Daddy said he would,
Then surely he will do.

This poet's faith is simple trust.
My Father's Word is true.
For Abba said He would,
And surely He shall do.

A Poetic Meditation of Luke 17:6 (AMPC)

And the Lord answered, If you had faith (trust and confidence in God) even [so small] like a grain of mustard seed, you could say to this mulberry tree, Be pulled up by the roots, and be planted in the sea, and it would obey you.

Conquest Armor

Believers wear white combat boots!
Their feet are fitly shod,
With the good news of God's peace . . .
On scorpions to trod.

These mighty men of valor,
Have put God's armor on;
They stand in faith as conquerors—
In victories made strong.

The belt of truth they've buckled,
Right snuggly to their waist;
While the breastplate of God's righteousness,
Glistens in its place.

Though fiery darts of demons hurled,
Are glancing off faith shields;
They fall to earth extinguished—
By the force of faith congealed.

In the Spirit at all times—alert!
They pray for all the saints.
They run beside swift horses—strong!
They walk and never faint.

While the helmet of salvation,
Guards their heart and mind;
With the sword of God's Spirit word,
They conquer as designed.

A Poetic Meditation of Ephesians 6:13–18 (AMPC)

Therefore put on God's complete armor, that you may be able to resist *and* stand your ground on the evil day [of danger], and, having done all [the crisis demands], to stand [firmly in your place].

Stand therefore [hold your ground], having tightened the belt of truth around your loins and having put on the breastplate of integrity *and* of moral rectitude *and* right standing with God,

And having shod your feet in preparation [to face the enemy with the firm-footed stability, the promptness, and the readiness produced by the good news] of the Gospel of peace.

Lift up over all the [covering] shield of saving faith, upon which you can quench all the flaming missiles of the wicked [one].

And take the helmet of salvation and the sword that the Spirit wields, which is the Word of God.

Pray at all times (on every occasion, in every season) in the Spirit, with all [manner of] prayer and entreaty. To that end keep alert and watch with strong purpose *and* perseverance, interceding in behalf of all the saints (God's consecrated people).

Faith for Victory

We have God's faith for victory.
Our Father helps us win.
For by the blood of God the Son,
We have been born again.

No longer by allegiance bound,
To Lucifer the thief,
We yield our living now to God,
Who gave to us relief.

We stumble not in darkness blind.
Deceiver holds no sway.
For we by blood of God the Son,
Are children of the day.

Our faith is not our faith alone.
God lends us His on earth.
The win we wield belongs to Him,
Who gave to us new birth.

A Poetic Meditation of 1 John 5:4 (AMPC)

For whatever is born of God is victorious over the world; and this is the victory that conquers the world, even our faith.

Faith in God

Faith in God is Bible faith.
It knows God's Word is true.
Faith in God is faith assured,
In what the Lord will do.

Faith in God has all the facts,
From cross to Easter morn.
Faith knows the devil's kingdom lost,
That day of the Firstborn.

Faith in God declares on earth,
The truth that Jesus won;
Speaks to mountains 'til they move,
Just like the Lord has done.

Have the faith of God today—
Obey our Lord's command.
Speak your faith, and faith will win,
As on God's Word you stand.

A Poetic Meditation of Mark 11:22 (AMPC)

And Jesus, replying, said to them,
Have faith in God [constantly].

Faith Is . . .

Faith is trust in God our friend.
Faith is walking hand in hand,
Down the paths where Father leads,
While trusting Christ to meet our need.

Faith is leaning on God's Word.
Faith is doing that we've heard,
From our Lord who faithful reigns,
And holds each pledge above His name.

Faith is trusting God to save.
Faith treads troubles looming grave,
Proving false the doubts that speak,
"Perhaps today God's love is weak!"

Faith is trust in God above.
Faith makes choice to share God's love,
That men may know redemption's plan;
And through our love, firmly grasp His hand.

A Poetic Meditation of Hebrews 11:1 (AMPC)

Now faith is the assurance (the confirmation, the title deed) of the things [we] hope for, being the proof of things [we] do not see *and* the conviction of their reality [faith perceiving as real fact what is not revealed to the senses].

Famed-Faith Epitaph

In Hebrews men are mentioned well,
Because by faith they stood . . .
Knowing all that God had said,
He would to them make good.

By faith is said of Abel's life . . .
Enoch's and Noah's too.
Abraham-Isaac-Jacob faith,
Declares God's Word is true.

And Sarah likewise stood in faith,
As Joseph and Moses did;
And faith set free from harlotry,
When Rahab two spies hid.

Gideon, Barak, Samson, Jephthah,
David, Samuel, and prophets . . .
All understood God's Word was good—
And gained God's famed-faith epitaph.

A Poetic Meditation of Hebrews 11:1–33 (AMPC)

Now faith is the assurance (the confirmation, the title deed) of the things [we] hope for, being the proof of things [we] do not see *and* the conviction of their reality [faith perceiving as real fact what is not revealed to the senses].

For by [faith—trust and holy fervor born of faith] the men of old had divine testimony borne to them *and* obtained a good report.

By faith we understand that the worlds [during the successive ages] were framed (fashioned, put in order, and equipped for their intended purpose) by the word of God, so that what we see was not made out of things which are visible.

[Prompted, actuated] by faith Abel brought God a better and more acceptable sacrifice than Cain, because of which it

was testified of him that he was righteous [that he was upright and in right standing with God], and God bore witness by accepting *and* acknowledging his gifts. And though he died, yet [through the incident] he is still speaking.

Because of faith Enoch was caught up *and* transferred to heaven, so that he did not have a glimpse of death; and he was not found, because God had translated him. For even before he was taken to heaven, he received testimony [still on record] that he had pleased *and* been satisfactory to God.

But without faith it is impossible to please *and* be satisfactory to Him. For whoever would come near to God must [necessarily] believe that God exists and that He is the rewarder of those who earnestly *and* diligently seek Him [out].

[Prompted] by faith Noah, being forewarned by God concerning events of which as yet there was no visible sign, took heed *and* diligently *and* reverently constructed *and* prepared an ark for the deliverance of his own family. By this [his faith which relied on God] he passed judgment *and* sentence on the world's unbelief and became an heir *and* possessor of righteousness (that relation of being right into which God puts the person who has faith).

[Urged on] by faith Abraham, when he was called, obeyed and went forth to a place which he was destined to receive as an inheritance; and he went, although he did not know *or* trouble his mind about where he was to go.

[Prompted] by faith he dwelt as a temporary resident in the land which was designated in the promise [of God, though he was like a stranger] in a strange country, living in tents with Isaac and Jacob, fellow heirs with him of the same promise.

For he was [waiting expectantly and confidently] looking forward to the city which has fixed *and* firm foundations, whose Architect *and* Builder is God.

Because of faith also Sarah herself received physical power to conceive a child, even when she was long past the age for it, because she considered [God] Who had given her the promise to be reliable *and* trustworthy *and* true to His word.

So from one man, though he was physically as good as dead, there have sprung descendants whose number is as the stars of heaven and as countless as the innumerable sands on the seashore.

These people all died controlled *and* sustained by their faith, but not having received the tangible fulfillment of [God's] promises, only having seen it *and* greeted it from a great distance by faith, and all the while acknowledging *and* confessing that they were strangers *and* temporary residents *and* exiles upon the earth.

Now those people who talk as they did show plainly that they are in search of a fatherland (their own country).

If they had been thinking with [homesick] remembrance of that country from which they were emigrants, they would have found constant opportunity to return to it.

But the truth is that they were yearning for *and* aspiring to a better *and* more desirable country, that is, a heavenly [one]. For that reason God is not ashamed to be called their God [even to be surnamed their God—the God of Abraham, Isaac, and Jacob], for He has prepared a city for them.

By faith Abraham, when he was put to the test [while the testing of his faith was still in progress], had already brought Isaac for an offering; he who had gladly received *and* welcomed [God's] promises was ready to sacrifice his only son,

Of whom it was said, Through Isaac shall your descendants be reckoned.

For he reasoned that God was able to raise [him] up even from among the dead. Indeed in the sense that Isaac was figuratively dead [potentially sacrificed], he did [actually] receive him back from the dead.

[With eyes of] faith Isaac, looking far into the future, invoked blessings upon Jacob and Esau.

[Prompted] by faith Jacob, when he was dying, blessed each of Joseph's sons and bowed in prayer over the top of his staff.

[Actuated] by faith Joseph, when nearing the end of his life, referred to [the promise of God for] the departure of the Israelites out of Egypt and gave instructions concerning the burial of his own bones.

[Prompted] by faith Moses, after his birth, was kept concealed for three months by his parents, because they saw how comely the child was; and they were not overawed *and* terrified by the king's decree.

[Aroused] by faith Moses, when he had grown to maturity *and* become great, refused to be called the son of Pharaoh's daughter,

Because he preferred to share the oppression [suffer the hardships] *and* bear the shame of the people of God rather than to have the fleeting enjoyment of a sinful life.

He considered the contempt *and* abuse *and* shame [borne for] the Christ (the Messiah Who was to come) to be greater wealth than all the treasures of Egypt, for he looked forward and away to the reward (recompense).

[Motivated] by faith he left Egypt behind him, being unawed *and* undismayed by the wrath of the king; for he never flinched *but* held staunchly to his purpose *and* endured steadfastly as one who gazed on Him Who is invisible.

By faith (simple trust and confidence in God) he instituted *and* carried out the Passover and the sprinkling of the blood [on the doorposts], so that the destroyer of the firstborn (the angel) might not touch those [of the children of Israel].

[Urged on] by faith the people crossed the Red Sea as [though] on dry land, but when the Egyptians tried to do the same thing they were swallowed up [by the sea].

Because of faith the walls of Jericho fell down after they had been encompassed for seven days [by the Israelites].

[Prompted] by faith Rahab the prostitute was not destroyed along with those who refused to believe *and* obey, because she had received the spies in peace [without enmity].

And what shall I say further? For time would fail me to tell of Gideon, Barak, Samson, Jephthah, of David and Samuel and the prophets,

Who by [the help of] faith subdued kingdoms, administered justice, obtained promised blessings, closed the mouths of lions.

Feeling and Faith

Feeling and faith seldom share,
An increment of time.
When you're feeling a million bucks,
Your faith may be a dime.

It's possible the two could share,
But not especially so.
With your feeling you think it is,
But by your faith, you know.

Faith is based on knowledge of,
God's eternal Word.
Feeling comes and goes again,
Swayed by what you've heard.

Faith is now—this moment.
Faith says, "It is this hour."
Faith stands tall; but feeling crawls,
For feeling has no power.

Today you feel God cares for you;
Tomorrow . . . that He's forgot.
Feeling wonders if God left;
Faith knows your God has not.

When next you need an answer,
Your feelings please remind,
"God is forever faithful;
Not sometimes deaf and blind."

When with your feelings you seek God,
You have an endless quest.
Looking and a wishing for,
What faith knew you possessed.

So keep your spirit richly fed,
And on God's Word depend.
Feeling only hangs around . . .
Faith is your trusting friend.

A Poetic Meditation of Mark 11:23, Hebrews 11:1 (AMPC)

Truly I tell you, whoever says to this mountain, Be lifted up and thrown into the sea! and does not doubt at all in his heart but believes that what he says will take place, it will be done for him.

Now faith is the assurance (the confirmation, the title deed) of the things [we] hope for, being the proof of things [we] do not see *and* the conviction of their reality [faith perceiving as real fact what is not revealed to the senses].

Giant Killer Faith

Let your faith be a giant killer—
Like David speak your heart.
Tell aloud what God will do,
And watch your doubts depart.

Look beyond your giant fears,
To see life as God sees.
You are your Lord's. Declare His Word,
And giant fears will flee.

Cast out the giants in your life;
By faith decree their fate.
All the might of angel hosts,
On faith-filled speaking wait.

Faith speaks, declares, decrees, then joys,
In what the Lord has done.
Like David of old you must speak bold.
Faith takes what Jesus won.

A Poetic Meditation of 1 Samuel 17:36–37 (AMPC)

Your servant killed both the lion and the bear; and this uncir-
cumcised Philistine shall be like one of them, for he has defied
the armies of the living God! David said, The Lord Who delivered
me out of the paw of the lion and out of the paw of the bear, He
will deliver me out of the hand of this Philistine. And Saul said to
David, Go, and the Lord be with you!

Giants in the Land

These are My giants in the land—
My mighty warfare sons—
Clothed in My Spirit armor,
For victories I won.

Looking to My wisdom,
Listening to command,
Their purpose is a harvest scythe,
Sweeping through the land.

Each kernel gleaned is harvest yield,
From watered seeds of Word;
For every intercessory prayer,
The Holy Spirit heard.

Take the cities by My blood,
Restore the broken, maimed;
Every battered cast-down one,
My Holy Spirit claims.

A Poetic Meditation of Hebrews 7:25 (AMPC)

Therefore He is able also to save to the uttermost (completely, perfectly, finally, and for all time and eternity) those who come to God through Him, since He is always living to make petition to God *and* intercede with Him and intervene for them.

Give

When you give of yourself,
To the weak and oppressed,
You are lending to God,
And your life He will bless.

For each gift you bestow,
The Lord in His grace,
Gives treasures of mercy,
Your loss to erase.

So give from God's blessing—
Your heart opened wide—
And Jehovah Lord Jireh,
Your need will provide.

A Poetic Meditation of Proverbs 19:17 (AMPC)

He who has pity on the poor lends to the Lord, and that which he has given He will repay to him.

Hear Our Father Cry

When praying in the Spirit,
We hear our Father cry:
"Take to men My words of life;
Don't let the lost ones die!

"That you might lead from darkness,
To heaven's love and light,
Is that for which you're purchased.
Now rise to join the fight.

"To Spirit truth awaken—
At stake the souls of men.
And when one dies without My Son,
The devil laughs again.

"And who believes in heaven,
If they've not seen My power?
And as you fail to live My love,
The flames of hell devour.

"What greater proof of heaven,
Than heaven in My own.
Your world will pause to listen,
When they behold My throne.

"My throne is delegated might;
My power is love displayed.
Dominion flows through hearts of love,
Who have My plan obeyed.

"Come, linger in My presence,
Bow to My Spirit there.
Abide in Me—My words in you—
Then rise to live your prayer."

A Poetic Meditation of 1 Corinthians 14:15 (AMPC)
Then what am I to do? I will pray with my spirit [by the Holy Spirit that is within me], but I will also pray [intelligently] with my mind *and* understanding; I will sing with my spirit [by the Holy Spirit that is within me], but I will sing [intelligently] with my mind *and* understanding also.

Heaven's Hometown Bank

As a family member,
With abundant life provision,
Will you take your place—
Your blood-won position?
The Lamb's blood cleansed you.
When living water you drank.
Now you are accepted,
At Heaven's Hometown Bank.

Windows are open wide,
To serve the sons of men.
The bank with Jesus's signature,
Will never close again!
For He reigns in love and might,
Abundant life to bring,
To all who claim God's written Word,
As will of Christ their King.

Those who know the Son of God,
As Rapha-Jireh Lord,
Know they are the sons of God,
And heirs through His Word.
To all His love promises,
They cling when they feel want;
Standing firm, eyes faithfully fixed,
On their New Covenant.

For Father's First-Time Covenant,
Had coverage truly wide,
But new means new and better,
And none will be denied.
For all born new by sacrifice,
Of Jesus's cleansing blood,
Have sonship rights, with access to,
Heaven's blessing flood.

A Poetic Meditation of John 10:10 (AMPC)

The thief comes only in order to steal and kill and destroy. I came that they may have *and* enjoy life, and have it in abundance (to the full, till it overflows).

Heaven's Victory

Without prayer no victory,
Would Christ have won on earth—
It was in prevailing agony,
The Lord His death gave birth:

"Father, not My will but Yours,
For You, My God, are Lord;
Now in My flesh Your love express,
According to Your Word."

And as He chose redemption's plan,
Vile Hades-clones would soon quake;
Christ's prayer prevailed for all mankind—
The chains of sin to break.

"Father, Your will is My choice!"
Birthed heaven's victory;
And from His night of groaning prayer,
There glows the dawn we see.

A Poetic Meditation of Luke 22:44 (AMPC)

And being in an agony [of mind], He prayed [all the] more earnestly *and* intently, and His sweat became like great clots of blood dropping down upon the ground.

Her Chamber Song

When victories come that Jesus won,
His praise rewards the fight!
As deep blood-sweating groans prevail,
His joy bursts bright the night.

Christ saw this day rejoicing,
For the warring Bride He birthed.
She sends hell's host to route,
Retreating beneath His Word.

This conquest Bride of Mercy,
Gives birth by writhing prayer.
And toiling in her chamber song,
His righteous work declares.

On her knees she worships,
Her Sovereign Prince of Zion.
In glistening robes, His diamond rare,
Gives mirth to Judah's Lion.

A Poetic Meditation of Luke 22:44 (AMPC)

And being in an agony [of mind], He prayed [all the] more earnestly *and* intently, and His sweat became like great clots of blood dropping down upon the ground.

His Robe, His Sword, His Shield

God gave a robe—a righteous robe—
In blood of Christ washed clean;
God gave His robe, His sword, His shield;
I'm mighty in my King.
I win o'er wrong, to lift in song,
The victory Christ brings.

A Poetic Meditation of Ephesians 6:16–17 (AMPC)
Lift up over all the [covering] shield of saving faith, upon which you can quench all the flaming missiles of the wicked [one]. And take the helmet of salvation and the sword that the Spirit wields, which is the Word of God.

Honest? Doubt

I've never known an honest doubt,
For at their root this lie,
"God does not do what He's declared,
And will not hear your cry."

Doubts are tools to destruct faith—
They've demon origin—
For Satan was the first to speak,
"God did not say nor mean."

Dishonest doubts, the only breed;
So cast them down this day.
With honest words of faith proclaim,
"God says, '. . .!' and you can't stay!"

A Poetic Meditation of Luke 12:29 (AMPC)

And you, do not seek [by meditating and reasoning to inquire into] what you are to eat and what you are to drink; nor be of anxious (troubled) mind [unsettled, excited, worried, and in suspense].

Interceding Advocate

In Father's Throne Room Court,
Our advocate Christ is.
God understands by blood we stand,
And justice to us gives.

Though tempter-deceiver-slanderer,
To God recites our sins,
Lord Jesus Christ, our advocate,
Says, "By My blood they win!"

Our attorney
"Summary judgment!" pleads.
(Though the evil one protests),
And gavel falls as Lord of All—
Our Dad—grants our request.
[Not guilty of their sins!
In Christ, forgiveness meted!
Their request is from
Your Word our God!
Promised-provision . . . granted!

Worthy! Once again, they have come,
Through the blood of God, the Son!]

A Poetic Meditation of Hebrews 7:25 (AMPC)

Therefore He is able also to save to the uttermost (completely, perfectly, finally, and for all time and eternity) those who come to God through Him, since He is always living to make petition to God *and* intercede with Him *and* intervene for them.

Intercessory Prayer

Jesus is your friend divine;
He died to make you free.
Now He reigns in power and love,
Throughout eternity.

Ascended to His Father,
There seated on His right,
He's pleading now for blood-bought sons,
That they might walk in light.

Your advocate to Father's heart,
In intercessory prayer,
Pleads for you unceasingly.
Bow to meet Him there.

With Jesus join in entreaty,
That saints by sin maligned,
Will sins forsake to be restored,
In Father's grace divine.

A Poetic Meditation of Hebrews 7:25 (AMPC)

Therefore He is able also to save to the uttermost (completely, perfectly, finally, and for all time and eternity) those who come to God through Him, since He is always living to make petition to God *and* intercede with Him *and* intervene for them.

Jehovah God the Son

Three men stood while others bowed,
Yet four men all men viewed.
For in the heat of seven times,
The Fourth was like unto . . .

The Son of God, the Son of Man—
Messiah in the old.
They would not bow, nor would their God;
He came as they foretold!

"Our God is able, and He shall,
Deliver from death's door.
This image formed of heathen gold,
Shall bow to Evermore."

By the faith of their confession,
The Hebrew three had won.
The Fourth was their Deliverer—
Jehovah God . . . the Son!

A Poetic Meditation of Daniel 3:9, 24–25 (AMPC)

They said to King Nebuchadnezzar, O king, live forever! Then Nebuchadnezzar the king [saw and] was astounded, and he jumped up and said to his counselors, Did we not cast three men bound into the midst of the fire? They answered, True, O king. He answered, Behold, I see four men loose, walking in the midst of the fire, and they are not hurt! And the form of the fourth is like a son of the gods!

Living Faith

Faith that will not follow,
Is faith that's fallen dead;
But faith that goes is living,
And works by love as said.

Faith demands our action,
His living faith to be;
Faith commands commitment now,
To heaven's Majesty.

Faith now lives in children,
Who feast on Father's Word,
And walk in love . . . surrendered,
To Jesus Christ their Lord.

A Poetic Meditation of Ephesians 2:8 (AMPC)

For it is by free grace (God's unmerited favor) that you are saved (delivered from judgment *and* made partakers of Christ's salvation) through [your] faith. And this [salvation] is not of yourselves [of your own doing, it came not through your own striving], but it is the gift of God.

Look to God

A vision "in the valley" comes,
By looking to the Lord;
Bringing from God's Spirit realm,
God's manifested Word.

While hidden in your heart, it's hope;
By vision faith is born.
Counting it done in God the Son;
Through patience it is formed.

When "in the valley," look to God;
It ain't His choice you're there.
Embrace God's best, and then confess,
His promise in your prayer.

Don't beg from God—it's not His style,
To keep His best from you—
But thank Him for the thing desired,
And count His promise true.

A Poetic Meditation of John 10:10 (AMPC)

The thief comes only in order to steal and kill and destroy. I came that they may have *and* enjoy life, and have it in abundance (to the full, till it overflows).

Love Signs

Go to your world good news to preach:
"I make of men new creatures!"
And as you go expect love signs,
To follow as My feature.

In My name cast out demons;
By My Spirit speak new tongues.
Lay your hands upon the sick;
To My name disease succumbs.

I'm Jesus Christ your victory!
In My name go this day.
Baptize the repenting,
For My blood has made the way.

Speak total restoration love!
I'm the healing love they yearn!
And as you go My love to share,
My might shall love confirm!

A Poetic Meditation of Mark 16:17–18 (AMPC)

And these attesting signs will accompany those who believe: in My name they will drive out demons; they will speak in new languages; They will pick up serpents; and [even] if they drink anything deadly, it will not hurt them; they will lay their hands on the sick, and they will get well.

The Marriage Supper Greeting

My friends, My faithful servants,
You obeyed our Father's will;
When in His might you fought the fight,
His purpose to fulfill.

His kingdom came to earth by you,
So faithful to His plan;
And here today—His will obeyed—
His ransomed host you stand.

My broken body made you whole,
My crimson washed you white;
So enter now into the feast,
In wedding garments bright.

Yes! Welcome home, My faithful Bride;
Our marriage supper eat . . .
Here in My father's kingdom,
Communion is complete.

A Poetic Meditation of Revelation 19:9 (AMPC)

Then [the angel] said to me, Write this down: Blessed (happy, to be envied) are those who are summoned (invited, called) to the marriage supper of the Lamb. And he said to me [further], These are the true words (the genuine and exact declarations) of God.

Testimony

In a Gaston, Oregon, house,
Our Savior's plea was made.
In answer to that call,
A simple prayer was prayed.

Daddy was the preacher,
Of a humble sermonette.
Responding to God's call,
This child Dad's Savior met.

Bowing at a chair,
An altar there we made,
As son and dad together,
To their Father prayed.

Our Father heard my prayer—
A contrite sinner's plea.
As I asked in Jesus's name,
God took my sin from me.

And that's the special reason,
I share these poems with you;
That you might choose to make,
My Lord your Savior too.

A Poetic Meditation of Romans 10:9 (AMPC)

Because if you acknowledge *and* confess with your lips that Jesus is Lord and in your heart believe (adhere to, trust in, and rely on the truth) that God raised Him from the dead, you will be saved.